D1231559

6/18

COMMUNITY HELPERS

Nurses

by Christina Leaf

BELLWETHER MEDIA • MINNEAPOLIS, MN

Note to Librarians, Teachers, and Parents:

Blastoff! Readers are carefully developed by literacy experts and combine standards-based content with developmentally appropriate text.

Level 1 provides the most support through repetition of high-frequency words, light text, predictable sentence patterns, and strong visual support.

Level 2 offers early readers a bit more challenge through varied simple sentences, increased text load, and less repetition of high-frequency words.

Level 3 advances early-fluent readers toward fluency through increased text and concept load, less reliance on visuals, longer sentences, and more literary language.

Level 4 builds reading stamina by providing more text per page, increased use of punctuation, greater variation in sentence patterns, and increasingly challenging vocabulary.

Level 5 encourages children to move from "learning to read" to "reading to learn" by providing even more text, varied writing styles, and less familiar topics.

Whichever book is right for your reader, Blastoff! Readers are the perfect books to build confidence and encourage a love of reading that will last a lifetime!

This edition first published in 2018 by Bellwether Media, Inc.

No part of this publication may be reproduced in whole or in part without written permission of the publisher. For information regarding permission, write to Bellwether Media, Inc., Attention: Permissions Department, 5357 Penn Avenue South, Minneapolis, MN 55419.

Library of Congress Cataloging-in-Publication Data

Names: Leaf, Christina, author.
Title: Nurses / by Christina Leaf.
Description: Minneapolis, MN : Bellwether Media, Inc., [2018] | Series: Blastoff! Readers. Community Helpers |
    Includes bibliographical references and index. | Audience: Ages 5-8. | Audience: Grades K to 3.
Identifiers: LCCN 2017032148 (print) | LCCN 2017032330 (ebook) | ISBN 9781626177482
    (hardcover : alk. paper) | ISBN 9781681034492 (ebook)
Subjects: LCSH: Nurses–Juvenile literature. | Nursing–Juvenile literature.
Classification: LCC RT61.5 (ebook) | LCC RT61.5 .L43 2018 (print) | DDC 610.73–dc23
LC record available at https://lccn.loc.gov/2017032148

Editor: Nathan Sommer   Designer: Brittany McIntosh

Printed in the United States of America, North Mankato, MN.

Table of Contents

Time for a Shot

Maria holds her mom's hand. The nurse says the shot will barely hurt.

After, the nurse gives Maria a **bandage**. That was not so bad!

bandage

What Are Nurses?

Nurses care for sick and **injured** people. They keep **patients** healthy!

patient

Most nurses work in **hospitals** or **clinics**. Others work in schools or visit homes.

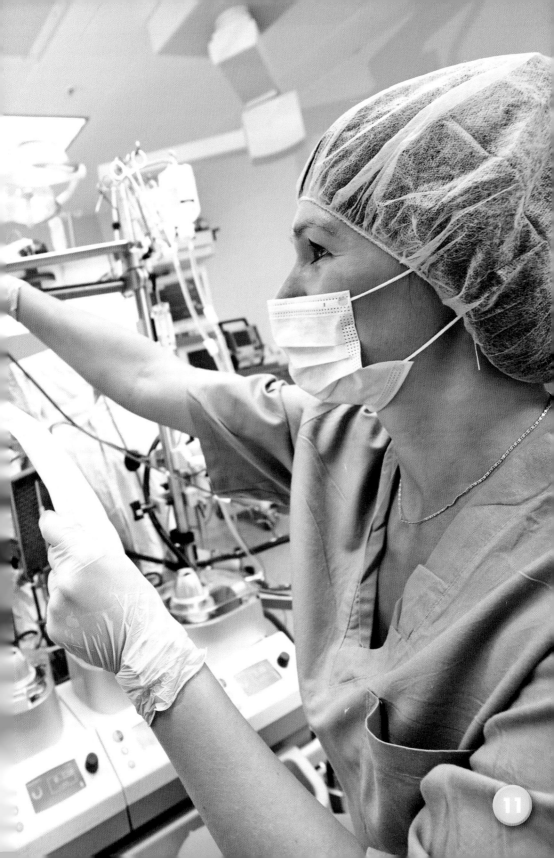

What Do Nurses Do?

Nurses check patient health. They look for signs of injuries and sicknesses.

Nurse Gear

scrubs   stethoscope   thermometer   blood pressure
monitor

13

Nurses give **medicine** to patients. Then they track how it changes their health.

medicine

Nurses often make care plans with doctors. They help patients understand the plans.

What Makes a Good Nurse?

Nurses listen carefully. They teach people how to care for themselves.

Nurse Skills

- ✓ good communicators
- ✓ friendly
- ✓ good listeners
- ✓ caring

19

Nurses are also caring. They help people get better!

Glossary

bandage

a covering used to heal cuts or breaks in skin

injured

hurt or unable to act because of harm to the body

clinics

places where people get checkups or other short medical visits

medicine

a drug used to treat sicknesses

hospitals

places where people receive emergency care or longer medical visits

patients

people in need of medical care

To Learn More

AT THE LIBRARY
Bell, Samantha. *Nurse.* Ann Arbor, Mich.: Cherry Lake Publishing, 2017.

Garrett, Winston. *What Does the School Nurse Do?* New York, N.Y.: PowerKids Press, 2015.

Parkes, Elle. *Hooray for Nurses!* Minneapolis, Minn.: Lerner Publications, 2017.

ON THE WEB
Learning more about nurses is as easy as 1, 2, 3.

1. Go to www.factsurfer.com.

2. Enter "nurses" into the search box.

3. Click the "Surf" button and you will see a list of related web sites.

With factsurfer.com, finding more information is just a click away.

Index

The images in this book are reproduced through the courtesy of: Tyler Olson, front cover; Suwin, pp. 2-3; asiseeit, pp. 4-5, 6-7; asiseeit/ Getty Images, pp. 8-9; Dmitry Kalinovsky, pp. 10-11; Hero Images/ Getty Images, pp. 12-13; EHStockphoto, p. 13 (scrubs); romiri, p. 13 (blood pressure monitor); onair, p. 13 (thermometer); ziviani, p. 13 (stethoscope); kali9, pp. 14-15; FS Stock, pp. 16-17; Terry Vine/ Getty Images, pp. 18-19; Monkey Business Images, pp. 20-21; Di Studio, p. 22 (top left); Marko Poplasen, p. 22 (center left); John Panella, p. 22 (bottom left); George Rudy, p. 22 (top right); siam.pukkato, p. 22 (center right); Air Images, p. 22 (bottom right).